People of the Bible

The Bible through stories and pictures

The First Easter

The First Easter

Retold by Catherine Storr
Pictures by Chris Molan

Franklin Watts Limited · London
in association with Belitha Press Limited · London

It was the time of the Passover.
Jesus knew that he was coming
to the end of his work in this world.
He told his disciples, Peter and John,
to go into Jerusalem,
where they would meet a man
carrying a pitcher of water.
When they found him, they asked
if Jesus and his disciples could celebrate
the Passover in his upstairs guest room.

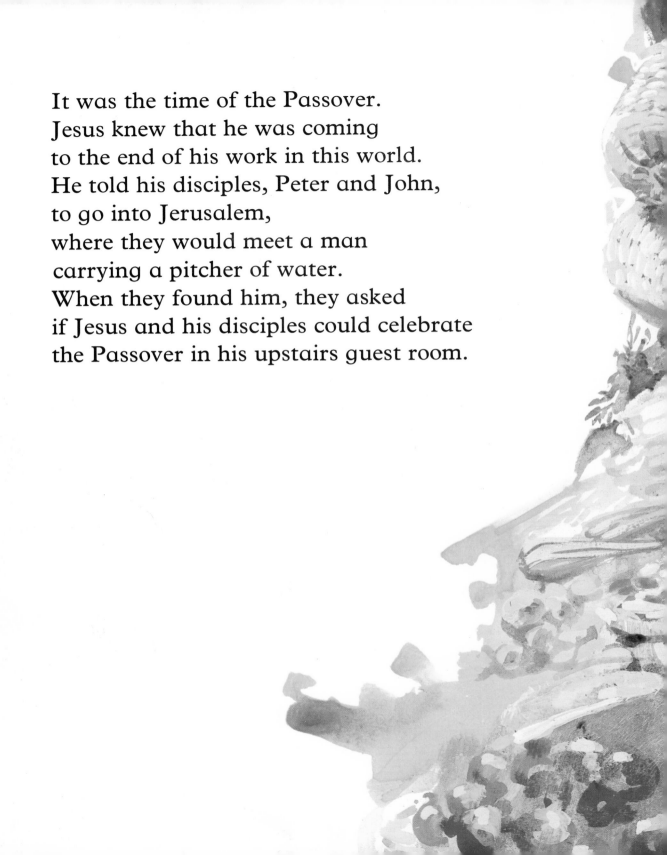

While they were eating the Passover supper
in the upper room, Jesus said, 'One of you
is going to betray me to my enemies,
the high priests and the Roman governor of the city.'

Each disciple asked, 'Is it me? Is it me?'
Jesus said, 'It will be the one who dips his hand with
me into the dish.' Jesus took bread and broke it.
Then he gave his disciples wine.
He said, 'Eat this bread, and drink this wine
in remembrance of me.'

After they had sung a hymn,
they all went out to the Mount of Olives.
Jesus told his disciples,
'Tonight you will all be in trouble because of me.'
Peter said, 'Everyone else may be in trouble,
but I'll always stand by you.'
But Jesus said,
'Before the cock crows tomorrow morning,
you will three times deny that you know me.'

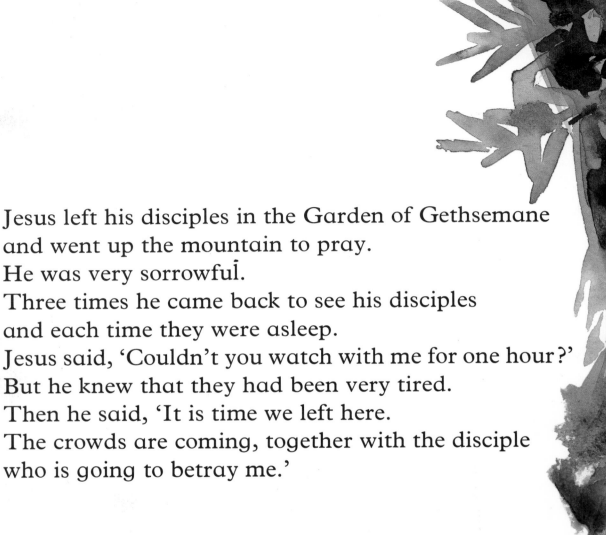

Jesus left his disciples in the Garden of Gethsemane
and went up the mountain to pray.
He was very sorrowful.
Three times he came back to see his disciples
and each time they were asleep.
Jesus said, 'Couldn't you watch with me for one hour?'
But he knew that they had been very tired.
Then he said, 'It is time we left here.
The crowds are coming, together with the disciple
who is going to betray me.'

It was Judas Iscariot who gave Jesus away
to the high priests and the elders.
They paid him thirty pieces of silver
to tell them where Jesus was.
Judas said to them,
'The man I shall greet with a kiss
is the man you want.'

When he saw Jesus, he said, 'Hail Master',
and kissed him.
At once, the people caught hold of Jesus,
to take him prisoner.

When he saw this,
Peter was angry and he drew his sword.
He cut off one man's ear.
But Jesus said, 'Put up your sword,
I don't need it. My father in heaven
could send twelve legions of angels
if I wanted to be kept safe.'
Then he healed the man's ear.

The crowd took Jesus to the house of Caiaphas,
the high priest. Many people came there
to swear that Jesus had pretended
to be the King of the Jews.
They said he had plotted against the Romans
who ruled the country.
While this was going on, Peter was outside.
A girl came up to him and said,
'You are a friend of that Jesus.'
Peter said, 'No, I don't know him.'
Then two more people said,
'You were with Jesus of Nazareth.'
Peter went on swearing that he wasn't,
when suddenly the cock crowed.
Peter remembered what Jesus had told him.
He went outside and wept bitterly.

In the morning, the high priests and elders
took Jesus to Pontius Pilate, the Roman governor,
to have him condemned to death. When Judas saw
this, he tried to pay back the thirty pieces of silver
to the high priests.
But they would not take them.
Judas felt so bad, because he knew
that Jesus had done nothing wrong,
that he went and hanged himself.

When Pontius Pilate saw Jesus, he asked,
'Are you the King of the Jews?'
Jesus said, 'Those are your words, not mine.'

Pilate asked him a great many questions, but he
could not find that Jesus had done anything wrong.
He said to the people, 'This man is innocent.
Shall I let him go?' But the people cried, 'No!
We would rather you released Barabbas, the robber.'

While Pilate was wondering what to do,
his wife sent him a message.
She said, 'Don't let this good man be killed.
I had a dream about him last night.'
But Pilate knew that the crowds of people
wanted him to set free Barabbas, the thief,
and not Jesus. He did not dare to go against them.
He washed his hands in front of them and said,
'I am innocent of the blood of this good man.'

Before they took Jesus outside the city
to be killed, the soldiers mocked Jesus.
They put a crown of thorns on his head
and gave him a purple robe,
and they pretended to worship him.
They whipped him and made him carry a wooden cross
to the place where he was to be crucified, Calvary.

Jesus was crucified between two thieves.
The soldiers taunted him.
They said, 'If you are the son of God,
get down off your cross.'
But Jesus prayed to God, 'Father, forgive them,
they don't know what they are doing.'
After three hours in the hot sun,
at last he died.

A man called Joseph of Arimathea
took Jesus' body to put in his own tomb.
He wrapped Jesus' body in linen and spices,
and rolled an enormous stone in front of the tomb
to keep the body safe.
Early the next morning,
Mary Magdalene went to the tomb
and found it empty.
The enormous stone had been rolled away.

Mary saw a figure in a long white robe
sitting in the tomb,
who asked her, 'Why do you cry?'
Mary said,
'Because they have taken away the body.'

She went out into the garden
and saw someone standing there,
whom she thought must be a gardener.
She asked him, 'Please, do you know
what has happened to Jesus' body?'
Then he said, 'Mary!'
She looked at him and saw it was Jesus,
come back from the dead.
She said, 'Master!' and was filled with joy.

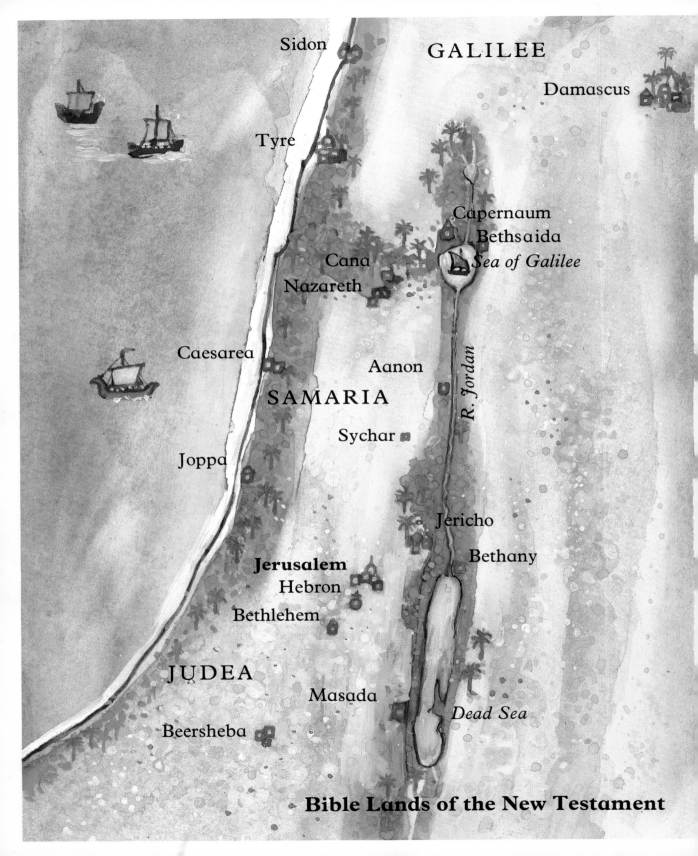

Bible Lands of the New Testament